My First Ballet Book

KINGFISHER

Kingfisher Publications Plc,
New Penderel House,
283–288 High Holborn,
London WC1V 7HZ
www.kingfisherpub.com

First published by Kingfisher
Publications Plc 2006
10 9 8 7 6 5 4 3 2 1

1TR/0606/LFG/CLSN/140MA/C

ISBN-13: 978 0 7534 1360 9
ISBN-10: 0 7534 1360 4

A CIP catalogue record for this book is available
from the British Library.

Printed in China

Senior editor: Catherine Brereton
Senior designer: Peter Clayman
Photographer: Richard Brown (www.richardbrown.photographer.com)
Wardrobe mistress and hair stylist: Lindsay Jackson
Picture research manager: Cee Weston-Baker
Senior production controller: Jessamy Oldfield
DTP manager: Nicky Studdart

Girls' practice clothes and shoes supplied by
Gamba Dancewear, London:
now in Paris: Repetto Paris, 22 rue de la Paix,
75002 Paris, France. 0800 91 70 395.
Costumes supplied by Lindsay Jackson.

Children from
The West London School of Dance:
www.thewestlondonschoolofdance.co.uk

Photographed at English National Ballet School:
www.enbschool.org.uk

Additional photography on page 32 and pages 42–45 by Joshua Tuifua
at the Royal Ballet, with kind permission of the Royal Ballet and dancers.

Note to readers: The website addresses listed in this book are correct
at the time of going to print. However, due to the ever-changing nature
of the internet, website addresses and content can change. Websites
can contain links that are unsuitable for children. The publisher cannot
be held responsible for changes in website addresses or content, or
for information obtained through third-party websites. We strongly
advise that internet searches should be supervised by an adult.

My First Ballet Book

Kate Castle

Ballet direction by
Anna du Boisson

KINGFISHER

Contents

What is ballet?

Ballet is a special way of dancing on stage. It is over 400 years old, and uses steps and movements, music, scenery and costumes to tell a story and fire up an audience's imagination. The movements take lots of practice to perfect, but ballet is fun to do and spectacular to watch.

The ballet teacher rehearses the students in the ballet studio.

When two people dance together in a ballet it's called a pas de deux or duet.

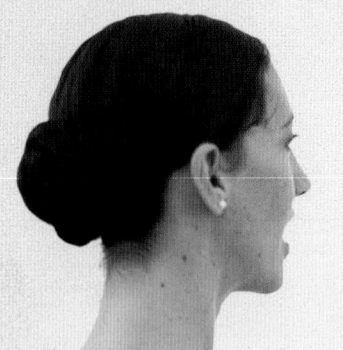

Costumes help create characters in a ballet, like these snowflakes.

Preparing to perform

These dancers are rehearsing for a production of *The Nutcracker*, a very popular ballet set to music by Tchaikovsky. It is often performed at Christmas.

Toy story

The Nutcracker is about a girl called Clara, who is given a magic nutcracker doll one Christmas. She travels to the Kingdom of Sweets, where she watches dances and meets the Sugar Plum Fairy.

Ready to dance

If you want to learn ballet, you will need to
find a good school and a qualified teacher.
As your muscles and bones are still growing,
you need to be taught properly and safely.
Dancing is a great way to exercise, and
you will meet new friends to dance with.

Be ready to listen
to the teacher and
dance your best.

Make sure you come to
class on time, wearing
your practice clothes.

Special clothes

You can buy ballet clothes and shoes at a dancewear shop. Shoes will need to be fitted properly and you can keep all your things in a special ballet bag.

Top tip

Checklist

Remember to bring:
- ballet practice clothes
- ballet shoes
- a hairbrush and comb
- for girls: hair pins, hair grips and perhaps a hairnet or hairband
- a bottle of water
- some fruit for energy
- a notebook and pencil so you can note down what you learn.

What to wear

Ballet practice clothes are designed so that you don't get too hot and you can move easily. They are close fitting so that the teacher can see clearly what your arms and legs are doing and can correct any mistakes. Many schools have special uniforms – one for girls and one for boys.

tidy hairstyle

leotard

practice skirt

pink tights

soft leather shoes

Tidy hair

Hair needs to be tidy and brushed off your face so the audience can see your expression, and so it won't get in your eyes.

Girls can tie their hair in plaits secured with pins and grips, use a hairband, or pin their hair into a bun or buns covered by a net.

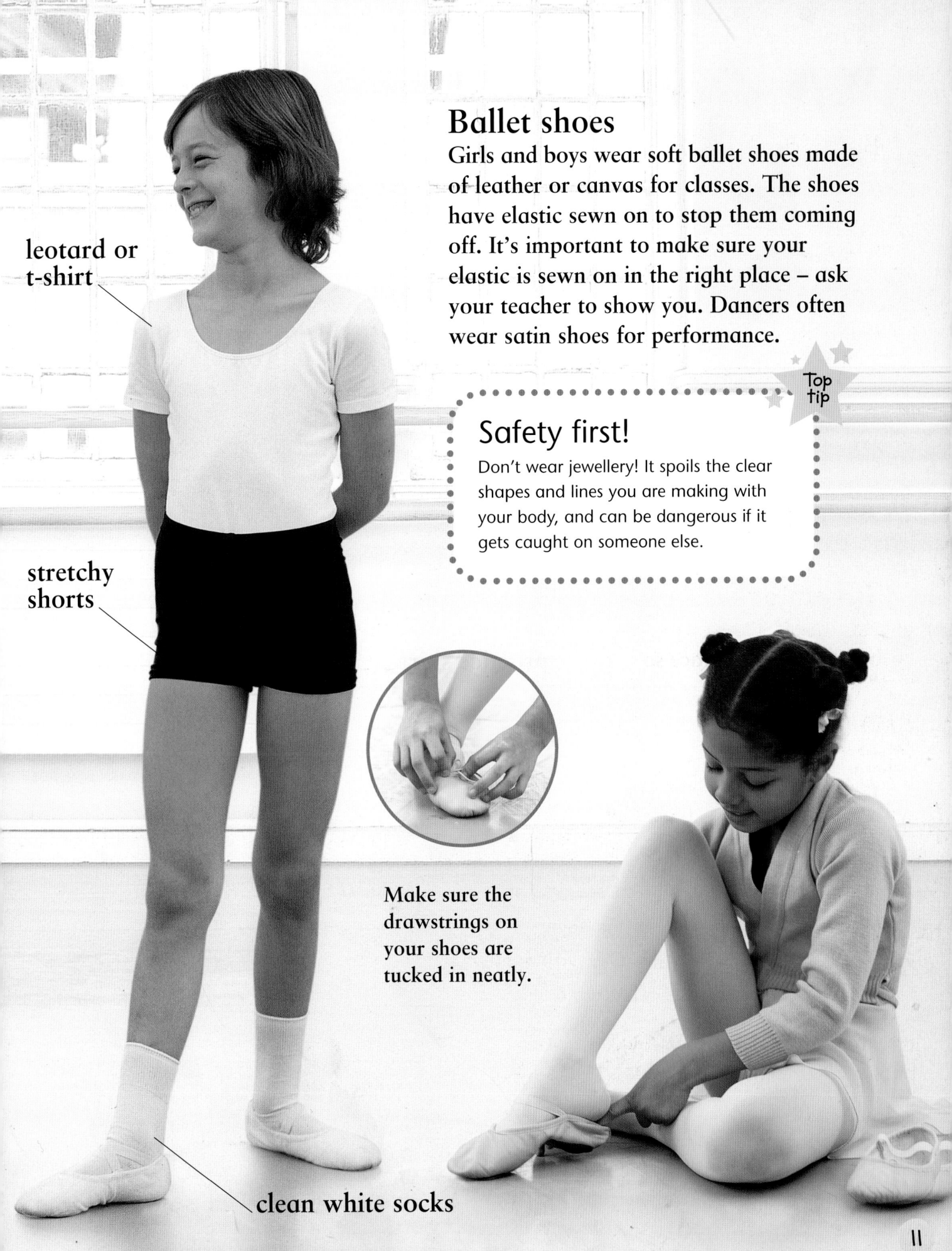

leotard or
t-shirt

stretchy
shorts

clean white socks

Ballet shoes

Girls and boys wear soft ballet shoes made
of leather or canvas for classes. The shoes
have elastic sewn on to stop them coming
off. It's important to make sure your
elastic is sewn on in the right place – ask
your teacher to show you. Dancers often
wear satin shoes for performance.

Top
tip

Safety first!

Don't wear jewellery! It spoils the clear
shapes and lines you are making with
your body, and can be dangerous if it
gets caught on someone else.

Make sure the
drawstrings on
your shoes are
tucked in neatly.

Ballet school

Ballet students and professional ballet dancers all practise in a studio like this. There are wooden handrails, called barres, around the walls, and mirrors so you can check that your positions are correct.

What to expect

Every class begins with a warm-up, followed by exercises at the barre. Then you come into the centre and put steps and movements together.

Top tip

Choosing a class

When you visit, check whether:
• the students look as if they're having fun
• there is room to dance properly
• the teacher is helping everyone to learn
• the music makes you want to dance
• you can dance in performances for friends and family.

barre

This practice tutu is worn by older students when they learn to dance with a partner.

These students are warming up before class begins.

12

Your teacher

The teacher will have passed examinations which mean he or she is allowed to teach dance. Sometimes the teacher will have been a professional dancer in a ballet company.

Teamwork
You can help each other by watching and talking about your dancing with your friends.

The teacher welcomes a new girl to the class.

The music

Without music, it would be difficult to dance in time – and less fun! Some schools use a pianist to play for classes, while others use a CD player.

The special floor is neither too hard nor slippery.

Warming up

All dancers need to stretch and warm up their muscles before they do class or perform on stage. This is to prevent injury. At the end of the class they will also cool down.

In this exercise you sit tall and flex and point your feet to develop strong insteps, which you need for jumping and dancing on your toes.

Turning out

Ballet students learn to turn out their legs by turning from the hip socket so that their knees face the side, not the front. This means they can raise their legs higher.

This Achilles stretch will help you jump higher.

This 'frog' position is to improve turn-out.

This exercise is for strengthening and loosening the inner thighs.

Get moving

After your stretches, it's time for some lively marching, skipping and running. These help the movements to flow and get the whole body working well.

This position strengthens your back.

This one stretches the hamstring muscles at the back of your thighs.

Top tip

On your own

Practise at home – a little bit each day. You can also show your friends at school how to warm up before PE lessons.

- Back stretch
- Hamstring stretch
- Tendon stretch
- Skipping, running and 'pony trots'
- 'Frogs' for turn-out (ballet only).

15

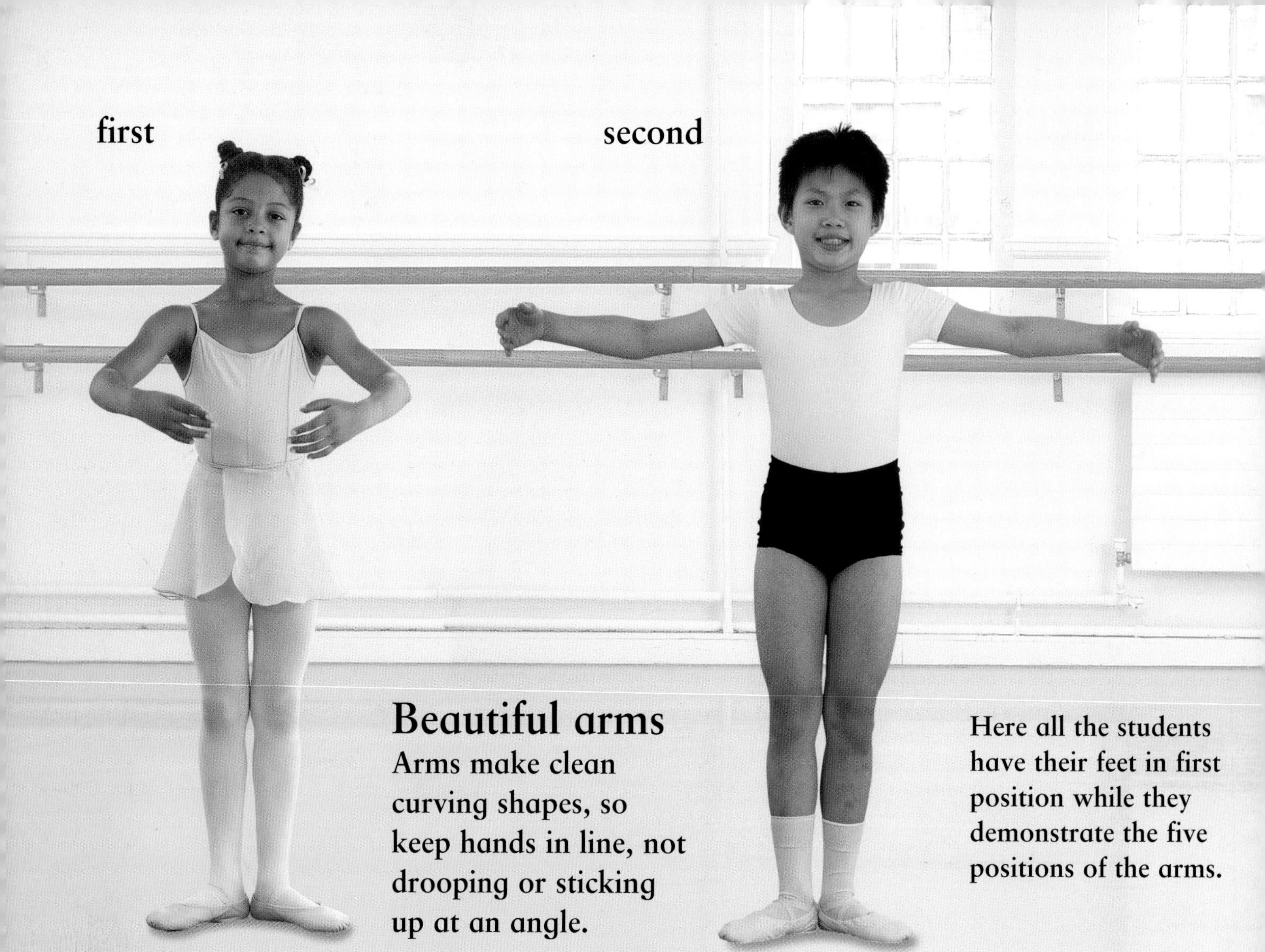

Beautiful arms
Arms make clean
curving shapes, so
keep hands in line, not
drooping or sticking
up at an angle.

Here all the students
have their feet in first
position while they
demonstrate the five
positions of the arms.

Arms and feet

There are five basic positions of the feet
and five for the arms. These are used in
lots of different combinations to make
beautiful, expressive positions. All ballet
movements begin and end in one of the
five feet positions. Enchaînements use
travelling, jumping and turning steps
in different combinations. Lots of
enchaînements make the solos, duets
and group dances that make a ballet.

Graceful hands
Your fingers
should be held
softly – not
clumped
together or spiky!

third　　　　　　**fourth**　　　　　　**fifth**

Top
tip

French words

Because ballet began in France, all the steps have French names. These are the basic movements.

- plier – to bend
- tourner – to turn
- sauter – to jump
- relever – to rise
- glisser – to glide
- étendre – to stretch
- élancer – to dart.

Neat feet

Although there are five positions of the feet, the ones dancers use most are second, fourth and fifth.

first

second
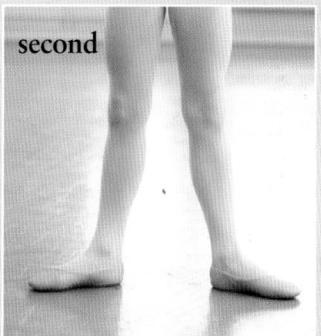

third

fourth
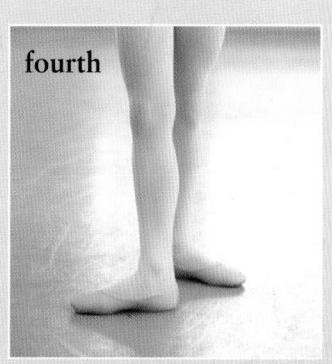

fifth

At the barre

The barre is your friend! It gives you support while you practise turning out your feet and legs. It helps you to stand straight and tall with all the parts of your body in line with each other.

Right and wrong

There are lots of things to remember at the barre, such as: stand straight, tummy in, shoulders level and arms and feet in the right place. Don't forget to breathe!

At the barre, don't grip or clutch the barre, like this...

but hold it lightly and firmly as if it's your partner.

To stand correctly, don't hunch your shoulders like this...

but stand tall – tummy pulled in, shoulders down.

Point your feet neatly, not pressed out of line in a sickle foot...

but pointed like this, with the foot straight to the side.

Fun for all

Anyone can learn to enjoy ballet, although not everyone wants to be a professional dancer. Ballet is a great way to keep fit and healthy, build confidence and develop your memory.

Top tip

Demi-plié in first position of the feet, at the barre, with arm in second.

Barre exercises

These students are stretching their feet in a movement called battement tendue devant. Devant means to the front. They will also practise pliés (bending) and relevés (stretches).

Relevé facing the barre. The children are stretching tall with feet in first, second and fifth position.

Here to help
The teacher helps with turn-out and alignment, so by the time you dance on stage you don't have to think about it.

Aiming higher

As you become older and stronger, you will be able to do more difficult exercises and feel as if you are really dancing. Even famous dancers still do their warm-up and barre exercises in a daily class which lasts for an hour and a half, before they even begin to rehearse or perform.

Arabesque penchée – which means tipped – with the arm in second position.

Arabesque
The arabesque is a beautiful position used in all ballets, and there are lots of different kinds.

Older girls do their exercises at the barre en pointe, like this relevé in the retiré position with the arm in fifth (left).

They do more difficult warm-ups too, like this stretching exercise for the back and hamstrings (right).

First arabesque – notice the turnout of the dancer's legs.

Arabesque à terre – on the ground. The legs are not quite so turned out, as this dancer is much younger.

Into the centre

After the barre exercises it's time to come into the centre. The studio is like the stage. Centre practice is about using the space so the audience sees your dancing from the best possible angle. Facing front is towards the audience.

In line

Exercises help you to make beautiful shapes in the space around you. This is called 'line' and means arms and legs making shapes that relate to each other in a way that is pleasing to look at.

This girl is doing a first arabesque, facing the corner of the studio, not the front.

Top tip

Step by step

In the centre, you'll learn:
- port de bras – flowing arm movements
- adage – slow movements for balance and stretching
- petit allegro – small neat jumps
- grand allegro – large travelling leaps.

The girls in the centre and right of the group are in croisé, or crossed, positions, facing opposite corners of the studio.

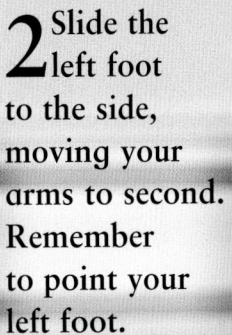

You can turn your back on the audience if your position has line and expression.

1 The pas de bourrée is a linking step. Begin in fifth position of the feet, and make a plié with arms in first.

2 Slide the left foot to the side, moving your arms to second. Remember to point your left foot.

3 Pull up into fifth position of the feet, in relevé, with your tummy in and your shoulders down.

4 Step to the side. Pas means step. Remember to focus towards the direction you are travelling.

5 Close into a plié again, with your head left. The sequence ends when you straighten your knees.

Spread your wings

Once you move away from the barre and into the centre you can really fly! Jumping, turning and travelling steps make ballet exciting to watch and fun to do. Practice at the barre gives you the strength and power you will need to do more difficult steps with ease.

Jumping high in the air is called 'elevation'. It takes strength and skill to make a clear shape like this.

Jumps – big and small

This dancer is leaping across the studio in a travelling jeté – which means 'to throw'. You can have fun with jumping and turning right from the beginning. Remember to point your toes as you jump.

1 This jump is called a petit changement or 'little change'. Begin in fifth position and make a demi-plié.

Taking off!

Begin with these little jumps or petits sautés. Start and finish in a demi-plié position. As you jump, remember to point your toes, keep your arms in position, shoulders down and body straight.

Top tip

Down and up

Before you can go up in the air you have to go down into the ground, so prepare for a jump with a good demi-plié. Don't throw your chest back as you jump, and make sure you put your heels on the ground as you land. Try to land softly and quietly, not with a big thump!

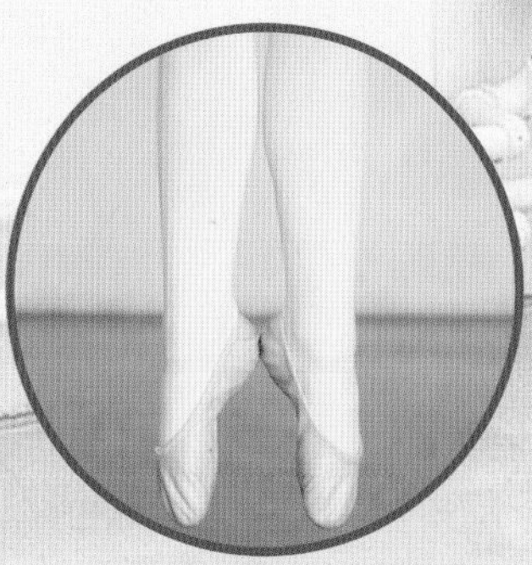

2 Spring in the air and change your feet over, bringing the back foot to the front, pointing your toes straight down.

3 Land softly, and you've completed the changement. If you like, try doing several of these jumps in a sequence.

Watching the older students helps inspire these children to become better dancers themselves.

Spinning around

You can start to turn by skipping and turning while travelling across the studio. It will take all the skills you have learnt so far – keeping head level, arms straight, shoulders down while still breathing and smiling!

Keep focussed

You need to focus as you do the skipping turn so you don't become giddy. Look at one spot and, just as you turn, whip your head round so you find the same spot again.

Top tip

Ways to turn

You can turn:
- in soft shoes
- en pointe
- on the spot
- travelling on one leg
- supported by a partner.

Why not try a spin yourself? Remember to focus on something so you don't get giddy.

Lots of turns

There are many different types of turns a dancer can learn, including pirouettes, posé turns and fouettés. The most difficult turns are the 32 fouettés danced by Odile in the ballet *Swan Lake*.

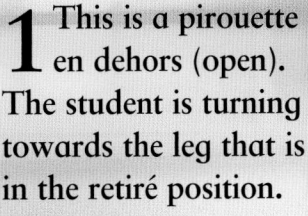

1 This is a pirouette en dehors (open). The student is turning towards the leg that is in the retiré position.

2 Turns require precision. The leg is perfectly turned out, so that the knee faces the side as she turns.

This dancer is in third position of the arms and fourth of the feet, ready to push off into a fast spin or pirouette.

This dancer is in the middle of a series of posé turns. Solos in ballets sometimes end with a series of these turns travelling very fast across the stage.

Dancing together

All ballets are made up of a combination of solos, duets and group dances. In a solo you dance alone, in a duet or pas de deux you perform with another dancer. Large groups are called the corps de ballet.

With a partner

Dancing in pairs takes skill. You have to remember the steps while dancing at the same time as your partner and in time to the music. You need to show you are enjoying dancing together, so making eye contact is important.

Keep your head straight as you dance shoulder to shoulder. Remember to point your toes as you skip!

This lift, called a pressage lift, is one of the most difficult in ballet and it requires great strength.

Dance groups

- Solo – dance for one
- Pas de deux – dance for two
- Pas de trois – dance for three
- Pas de quatre – dance for four
- Corps de ballet – large group.

Remember to point your toes, hold your tummy in, make the right shapes with your arms and legs, and smile!

Keep together

Watch the person next to you and try to keep perfectly together and in line when dancing this pas de trois – a dance for three.

This pas de deux is danced by older students. Use your finger to trace the lines and curves the dancers make with their bodies in the space around them.

29

On your toes

Dancing en pointe – on the tips of the toes – is something all young ballerinas look forward to. It makes turns look faster and more exciting, lengthens the legs so that positions look even more beautiful, and gives the impression that the dancer is very light, just skimming the ground.

Top tip

Safety first!

You can dance on your toes when:

- your legs and feet are strong enough
- your tummy muscles are strong enough
- you go to ballet class at least three times a week
- you are old enough (around 11 or 12)
- your teacher says you can.

Great strength

It takes a great deal of practice before a dancer's tummy and leg muscles are strong enough for dancing en pointe.

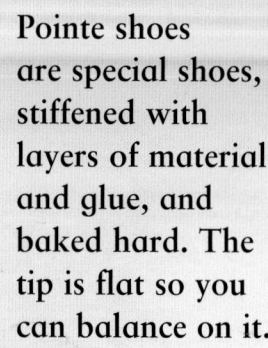

Pointe shoes are special shoes, stiffened with layers of material and glue, and baked hard. The tip is flat so you can balance on it.

Girls only

Only female ballet dancers dance on their toes. They will do all the same exercises and steps that the younger girls learn, like relevés and arabesques, but en pointe.

If you are taught properly, pointe shoes won't hurt your feet.

Pointe shoes need to be fitted properly. A professional ballerina may use up to 10 pairs of shoes a month.

Time to dance

Now the fun can begin! You know enough steps to enjoy that magic moment when music, costume and movement come together to make a ballet. The journey from studio to stage has begun. Change your practice clothes for a lovely costume and headdress, put on your best satin shoes and get ready to dance!

It takes years of practice to become a ballet star – the ballerina who dances the principal roles.

Team work

Ballet dancers know they are part of a team. Teachers, choreographers, musicians, designers and backstage staff are as important as the dancers, but they work behind the scenes.

Remember that even if you do become a star, you still need your friends to dance with!

Tutus

Ballerinas' dresses are called tutus. They are made of layers of net sewn onto a bodice trimmed with beads, ribbon, flowers, feathers or pretend jewels. Designing and making tutus and headdresses demands great skill.

Top
tip

Your ballet

First choose your story. Then find the right music. Make up the steps, called choreography. Design the scenery, costumes and make-up. You can draw posters to advertise your ballet, sell tickets and make programmes.

Music is used to create a mood or suggest a character and to paint pictures in the listener's mind. Listening will give you ideas for steps.

This class has decided to create a ballet about Alice in Wonderland.

Let's make a ballet

Most ballet schools put on performances where you can show what you have learned to friends and family. The audience will admire your skill, but above all you will be able to make them feel happy or sad, and tell stories with your dancing. You can make up ballets yourself and with friends, at home or in the ballet studio.

1 Invent steps for the story and characters, such as bunny hops for the White Rabbit.

2 Design your costumes and props. Costumes need to suggest the character but must be easy to dance in.

3 Put the finishing touches to your costumes. Use make-up to create the White Rabbit's nose and whiskers.

4 Perform your dance to the class. Here, Alice meets the White Rabbit. What are they telling you with their dancing?

35

From studio to stage

This ballet school is going to perform a ballet based on the well-known story, Peter Pan. The teacher has chosen the music, decided who will dance each character or role and choreographed the steps. It's time for rehearsals to begin.

These children (left) will be John, Michael and Wendy, the characters who fly to Neverland with Peter Pan.

The students find out which parts they will dance in the production.

The pianist will help the students rehearse their steps and dances.

Peter Pan and the fairy Tinkerbell are rehearsing their roles. You can see from her expression that Tinkerbell is angry with Peter Pan.

These boys are warming up during rehearsals. Part of the fun of dancing in a ballet production is meeting dancers from other classes.

Props

Objects dancers use on stage are called props – such as the teddy bear and sword used in this scene.

The teacher helps the children practise the steps until they can get them just right.

Practice makes perfect

After learning the steps, dancers will have many rehearsals in the studio and on stage before the ballet is danced in front of an audience. The dancers must remember the steps and dance them accurately, with expression and energy.

1 Dancers' costumes have been washed and ironed and are ready for them to collect. Dancers help each other into costume, making sure all fastenings are secure.

2 The soloists arrive and collect their costumes ready for the performance.

Ready to perform

There is one final rehearsal on stage in costume, called the dress rehearsal. Then the ballet is ready to be performed on stage for the audience. Dancers get ready and warm up backstage, and at last the curtain goes up! It's quite normal to feel a bit nervous on stage.

3 The dressing room is backstage at the theatre. Tidy hair is very important.

4 You need make-up or strong stage lighting will make your features seem to disappear!

The performance

Peter Pan dances with Tinkerbell, while John, Michael and Wendy look on. Each is wearing a costume and takes up a position that suggests their characters.

Top tip

Stage words

- Stage – where the ballet is performed
- Backstage – where dancers get ready, and costumes and scenery are stored
- Curtain – hides the stage
- Wings – where dancers enter and exit the stage.

Famous ballets

There are lots of famous ballets to enjoy. Some are based on fairy tales and magic and others on stories and plays. They fill the stage with movement, colour and music to delight audiences in theatres all over the world. You can watch ballet on TV and DVDs as well as going to see a professional performance.

The Firebird
Margot Fonteyn dances the role of the Firebird in this ballet based on a Russian fairy tale.

Musical dance
Not all ballets tell stories. *Elite Syncopations* uses colourful costumes and ragtime music by Scott Joplin to suggest all sorts of different moods, such as a funny duet for a tall and small dancer.

You will enjoy the ballet much more if you read the story before you go and listen to some of the music.

Giselle
This early ballet tells the story of a girl who falls in love with a prince in disguise.

The Nutcracker
The Prince dances a pas de deux with the Sugar Plum Fairy.

Sleeping Beauty
Many fairy tale characters dance at Princess Aurora's wedding.

Swan Lake
The black swan, Odile, pretends to be the Prince's true love, the white swan Odette.

The Dream
This ballet is based on Shakespeare's play *A Midsummer Night's Dream*. Enchanted creatures meet to cast their spells.

Behind the scenes

A dancer's day begins with class and ends with the performance. In between are rehearsals, costume fittings and, for principal dancers, coaching sessions. In a ballet company everyone is important and has a part to play in making sure the performance is the best it can possibly be.

Dancers rehearse in the studio wearing practice tutus and crossover cardigans.

Taking care

All dancers learn to take care of themselves by eating properly and getting enough rest. They also need to be organized to make sure they are always on time for class!

This dancer is checking her rehearsal schedule. She keeps warm with leg warmers and a tracksuit top, and has a bottle of water with her.

This dancer is wearing a leg warmer on an injured leg.

Top
Tip

Hard work

Dancing is as
demanding as any
sport or athletics.
Injured dancers have
physiotherapy or
massage to help
them recover.

Dancers usually put
on their own make-up.
For some roles a
special make-up is
designed as part of
the costume, and
make-up artists
are needed.

The dancers'
arms are in fourth
position as they
make a battement
tendue devant.

Dancers break in
new pointe shoes
in rehearsal, so they
are comfortable
and not too noisy.

Wardrobe staff look after and
repair costumes. Each dancer
must take care not to spill
anything on them, and to
hang them up properly.

At the ballet

At last – after all the preparation it's time for the ballet to begin. Everything comes together – dancing, music, scenery and costumes. So take your seat, watch, listen and enjoy as the curtain rises on the magical world of ballet.

Sleeping Beauty

In this scene, the Lilac Fairy blesses the baby Princess Aurora at her christening, while other fairies and courtiers look on. The shapes lead your eye to the most important people in the group – the Lilac Fairy and the baby princess.

Top tip

Enjoying ballet

Ask yourself some questions while you watch. What role would I like to dance? Do I know the names of any of the steps? How does the music help to tell the story? How does the choreographer use steps to make patterns? How did the ballet make me feel – happy, angry or sad?

Before the performance, musicians take their seats in the orchestra pit and the audience take their places. Then the ballet can start!

During the ballet, dancers watch a pas de deux from the wings as they wait to go on stage themselves. The audience sees it from a different angle.

At the end of the performance, dancers take a curtain call – their final curtsey and bow – and thank the audience for applauding.

Thank you!

Programmes tell you the story of the ballet and about the dancers. People sometimes send dancers flowers to show they enjoyed the performance.

Glossary

Adage (a-dahge)
Slow and sustained steps and movements which flow from one to another.

Alignment
Relationship of one part of the body to another.

Arabesque (ara-besk)
A position where the dancer balances on one leg with the other stretched and raised behind her.

Barre
A wooden rail, fixed to the walls of a dance studio. Dancers use it for balance as they practise basic exercises.

Choreographer
The person who has the idea for the ballet and then arranges the steps and patterns so that they make a whole.

Corps de ballet (core de ba-lay)
Dancers who perform together as a group and do not dance solos or leading roles.

Enchaînements (on-shane-mon)
A series of steps linked together, like words making a sentence.

En dehors (on day-ors)
Outwards from the supporting leg.

En pointe (on point)
Dancing on the tips of the toes in special stiffened shoes.

Étendre (eh-ton-dr)
To stretch.

Fouetté (fwe-tay)
A turn in which the working leg whips in a circular movement away from the supporting leg.

Glisser (glee-say)
To glide.

Grand allegro (gron a-leg-row)
Large jumping and travelling steps.

Grand jeté (gron she-tay)
A large travelling jump, with legs and arms outstretched.

Hamstring
One of five tendons at the back of the knee.

Line
The graceful shapes made by dancers' bodies in the space around them.

Orchestra pit
Where the musicians sit to play and the conductor stands to direct them during the performance.

Pas de bourrée (pah deh bou-ray)
Series of small linked travelling steps.

Pas de deux
(pah deh deh)
A dance for two people
in ballet.

Pas de trois
(pah deh twa) A dance for
three people in ballet.

Petit allegro
(petty a-leg-row)
Small jumping
and travelling steps
performed in
enchaînements.

Plié (plee-ay)
A basic ballet movement
in which the knees bend
and face the sides not
the front.

Props
Objects dancers use
in their hands on stage,
kept in the wings during
the performance.

Rehearsal
Practice session before
a performance.

Relevé (re-le-vay)
A rise on to the ball
of the foot.

Role
The part or character a
dancer plays in a ballet.

Sauter (soh-tay)
To jump.

Solo
A dance for one person.

Studio
The room where you learn
to dance, take daily class
and rehearse.

Turn-out
The way the dancer's
leg turns out from the
hip socket so that the
knees face the side.

Tutu
The ballerina's skirt,
made of many layers
of gathered net, which
can be very short
(classical) or
calf-length (romantic).

Wings
The space at the side of
the stage that the audience
can't see, where the
dancers wait to come on.

For more information
about classes contact:

Royal Academy of Dance
www.rad.org.uk

Imperial Society of
Teachers of Dancing
www.istd.org

British Ballet Organization
www.bbo.org.uk

and for performances
of ballet and other
forms of dance, contact
your local theatre
or dance agency.

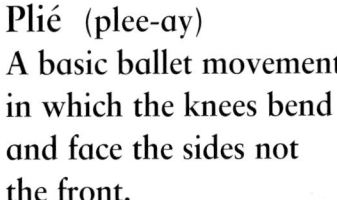

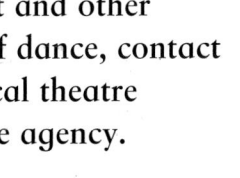

Index

Acknowledgements

The publisher would like to thank the following for their help in the production of this book:

Dancers: Leah Andreas, Curtis Angus, Helena Clark-Maxwell, Finn Cooke, Moesha Lamptey, Charlotte Levy, Helena Pratt, Kingsley Wong

The West London School of Dance: Kirsty Arnold, Anna du Boisson, Lindsay Jackson

English National Ballet School: Sue Preston

Photography: Richard Brown (www.richardbrownphotographer.com)

Royal Ballet: Joshua Tuifua (photography), Lauren Cuthbertson, Victoria Hewitt, Jonathan Howells, David Makhateli, Kristen McNally, Samantha Raine (dancers), Melanie Bouvet (ROH wig/make-up), Alisa Woodyard (ROH wardrobe)

Also Ann Burke, Vicky Bywater, Claire Cessford, Sheila Clewley, Russell Mclean and Jonathan Williams.

The publisher would like to thank the following for permission to reproduce their material. Every care has been taken to trace copyright holders. However, if there have been unintentional omissions or failure to trace copyright holders, we apologize and will, if informed, endeavour to make corrections in any future edition.
Pages 28*br* Alamy/Jeremy Hoare; 32*bl* Joshua Tuifua; 40*cl* Corbis/Robbie Jack; 40tr Getty/ Barron; 41*tl* Getty/AFP; 41*tlc* Topfoto/Performing Arts Library; 41*trc* Corbis/Robbie Jack; 41*tr* Corbis/Robbie Jack; 41*cr* Corbis/Robbie Jack; 42–43 all images Joshua Tuifua; 44*tr* Joshua Tuifua; 44–45*b* with the kind permission of English National Ballet, London; 45*l&r* Joshua Tuifua.